DEEP STATE
DEFECTOR IV

DEEP STATE DEFECTOR IV

Rahul Manchanda

To order additional copies of this book, contact:
Xlibris
844-714-8691
www.Xlibris.com
Orders@Xlibris.com
840302

CONTENTS

Chapter 1

The Hidden, Secret Agenda Behind The #MeToo Movement

The Founding Fathers/Pioneers of the United States of America risked life and limb to flee and escape from the bowels of Monarchial Europe, divided into little fiefdoms in the United Kingdom, Romania, France, Russia, Spain, Italy, Germany, Austria, etc, in order to get away from these Monarch's powers and abilities to detain the People at will, incarcerate them, torture them, murder them, stop them from working, destroy their families, rape/enslave their sisters, mothers and daughters, and gave themselves the ability to forge a new nation backed up by the Second Amendment with guns to maintain and keep their heard-earned freedoms of life, liberty and the pursuit of happiness, backed up, codified and guaranteed by the United States Constitution and the Bill of Rights.

Indeed, one of the hallmarks of criminal defense law and the punishments contained therein, is the establishment of guilt beyond a reasonable doubt, because such proceedings can result in the deprivation of a defendant's liberty or even in his or her death.

These outcomes are far more severe than in civil trials, in which money damages are the common remedy.

Clearly the founding of America in 1776 irked and irritated the Monarchy Powers of Europe (and the World) to no end, as they lost a major cash cow and source of revenue, not to mention that their illegitimate bastard children went on, with the fuel of freedom and personal autonomy, to evolve into the most powerful, richest and influential country in the world, effectively engulfing and rolling up Europe and its Monarchies within its breast and under its influence, globally.

The European Monarchies, having recognized that they could no longer bring back the citizenry of America under its foot again with bullets, guns and weapons (see the Battle of 1812, one of the last wars fought by and between European Monarchy (in this case the British) versus the American upstarts, who dared to go off on their own, decided to use subterfuge, trickery, buying off America's elected officials and judges to recruit a healthy generation of men and women who would willingly throw the protections afforded by the U.S. Constitution and Bill of Rights under the bus, exposing the American people to widespread and arbitrary arrest, incarceration, investigation, surveillance, murder and death if the powers that be, simply willed it to be so, just like it was for thousands of years before in Monarchial Europe (and the rest of world).

The Monarchies had learned long ago through stories involving men such as Martin Luther King and Mahatma Gandhi or even Steven Biko, that targeting/arresting men who had moral authority against their power only exposed their hidden hand, agenda, and undermined their entire program, so they immediately set about only going after men (and women) who the vast majority of the American people would find to be repulsive - their Patriot Act labeled their enemies "terrorists" while criminal prosecutions under the very well organized #MeToo movement being led by useful idiot communist fools such as irrational feminists, deranged and other gaggles of stupid short-sighted angry purple haired women who labeled their targets as "rapists" and "sexual assaulters."

But their agenda is the same - the wholesale removal of men and women from the protections and purview of the U.S. Constitution and Bill of Rights, simply by labeling a targeted citizen as such.

Harvey Weinstein, because he is a powerful wealthy and politically connected Jew, is a great target which proves that this is not a Zionist/Jewish agenda, but rather from their timeless and original Masters (European Monarchy) because if they can convict and destroy him, for alleged "crimes" that took place 10, 20, 30 years ago, with little to no evidence or corroboration, flying completely in the face of the "beyond a reasonable doubt" standard elucidated above, then they can get ***ANYBODY***, because complex sexual relationships by and between men and women, is as mainstream, normal and consistent with humanity as breathing air is.

His conviction would be a development that would effectively cancel the United States Constitution and Bill of Rights, i.e., end the United States of America completely, and the American people and most of its leadership/military/would not even have realized it.

This is what is known as a "Trojan Horse," recounting the story of the subterfuge that the Greeks used to enter the independent city of Troy and win the war.

In the canonical version, after a fruitless 10-year siege, the Greeks constructed a huge wooden horse, and hid a select force of men inside including Odysseus.

The Greeks pretended to sail away, and the Trojans pulled the horse into their city as a victory trophy.

That night the Greek force crept out of the horse and opened the gates for the rest of the Greek army, which had sailed back under cover of night.

The Greeks entered and destroyed the city of Troy, ending the war.

Metaphorically, a "Trojan Horse" has come to mean any trick or stratagem that causes a target to invite a foe into a securely protected bastion or place.

A malicious computer program that tricks users into willingly running it is also called a "Trojan horse" or simply a "Trojan."

The United States Constitution and its attendant Bill of Rights is not just some flimsy paper document that should be considered "cute" or "novel" or even "quaint," but rather should be acknowledged and reminded and remembered to be a written codification of inalienable human rights ordained by God, and not by Men, for which countless tens of million men and women have fought and died for, paying for these freedoms against tyranny with blood, sweat, tears, guts and their lives.

We may find men like Harvey Weinstein repulsive and repugnant to the infinite power, but this is the moral challenge and existential trap that these tyrannical monarchial money masters have set us up with - let's not forget that the U.S. Constitution and Bill of Rights protects everybody, not just men like Harvey Weinstein, Bill Cosby, and today's designated "terrorist of the day."

As German Lutheran pastor Martin Niemöller (1892–1984) stated in 1946, "First they came for the socialists, and I did not speak out—Because I was not a socialist. Then they came for the trade unionists, and I did not speak out—Because I was not a trade unionist. Then they came for the Jews, and I did not speak out—Because I was not a Jew. Then they came for me—and there was no one left to speak for me."

Chapter 2

Organized Witchcraft/Extreme Feminist Infiltration Of The American Family Courts

If someone were to come forward and provide evidence that American organized crime, particularly the Italian, Jewish, Chinese or Russian mafia controlled the federal and state courts of America, then clearly that issue would be aggressively investigated, those responsible prosecuted and jailed, and hopefully never would be repeated again as that would be criminal behavior, acts, public corruption, and conspiracy which, according to the FBI website "poses a fundamental threat to our national security and way of life."

The FBI website even goes on to get even more specific, stating that this type of public corruption affects "how verdicts are handed down in courts."

So why then, are open extremist feminists, often part of a closed network of Wiccan/Witch Covens of like-minded females, who take a blood oath to defend their coven/feminist/witchcraft network over and above the United States Constitution and all of its attendant laws, allowed to have completely taken over and infiltrated America's family courts, especially within the major cities of America?

Why has the FBI, Departments of Homeland Security and Justice, completely and totally ignored this rampant public corruption and collusion, which only permanently destroys and injures children, innocent men and fathers, and the families and businesses that depend on these destroyed individuals?

Well, under the guise of "protecting women," any type of criticism of this type of corruption automatically brands you as a misogynist, women or child abuser, or some other horrible appellation that has no bearing in truth or fact.

And the situation is even worse if the targeted man is a minority male who was involved with a white female member of this coven/extreme feminist/ organized witchcraft cabal, because then the full force of government persecution crushes his face like a jackboot, backed up by white men in federal and state law enforcement, the judiciary, the executive and legislative branches, to the point of complete and total absurdity *ad infinitum* into literal slavery.

Hopefully under the Trump administration, whose own nominees such as U.S. Supreme Court Judge Brett Kavanaugh were victims of this organized witchcraft/extreme feminist organized criminal conspiracy, will begin to dismantle and take apart this relatively unknown, under-reported, and shameful open criminal conspiracy operating right under the noses of law enforcement.

CHAPTER 3

Black People Can Also Be Racist Against Indians, Chinese, Muslims, Asians, White Women

Due to centuries of being kicked around by Whites, Blacks have developed a Post Traumatic Stress Disorder, and can be enormously racist against Indians, Chinese, Muslims and other Asians in America.

This is enormously scary because blacks are also dominant in U.S. Government positions because they generally prefer to become successful not in private companies or to start private businesses, so they are over-represented in U.S. Government employment, e.g., police officers, child protective service workers, judges, magistrates, immigration officers, postal workers, FBI agents, other types of government work where the person has a lot of power over peoples' lives.

So to that end, it is enormously scary when you have a bitter, angry, psychotic, and traumatized angry black racist in your face when you need to appeal for government assistance in any capacity.

These racist black people transform the USA into a completely and totally racist hell-hole against the relatively powerless Indians, Chinese, Muslims, Asians, and White Women.

Even poor White people (mostly White women) get the evil brunt of this Black racism each and every day from some of these imbalanced and racist Black American government employees.

This topic really needs to be discussed and dealt with, because most people are not even allowed to discuss it in public, while Black people generally deny that they can even **_be_** racist.

But again, since they are overwhelmingly dominant in U.S. Government job positions, some of them have transformed America into a racist hell-hole.

Chapter 4

President Trump's CEO Skills Are Coming In Handy During The Corona Virus War

On the night of March 22, 2020, President Donald J. Trump, flanked on his right by Vice President Mike Pence, and to his left by FEMA Administrator Peter Gaynor, appeared more in command and more Presidential than at any other time in his administration, as he professionally and mathematically rattled off in stark detail numbers relating to the Corona Virus and its effects on the United States of America.

His compassion, steadfastness, and direct leadership skills echoed images of Winston Churchill, and his bulldog spirit came through, loud and clear.

The administration of President Trump matured on this day, to become a Wartime President.

In this day and age, when warfare between nations has changed from outright artillery and bombs and fire, instead towards subterfuge, biological and chemical warfare and false flags, wherein he declared that the invisible enemy has attacked countless nations all at once, President Trump has vowed that we would defeat this enemy, offering his own hard-earned character, energy, optimism, strength, positivity, and leadership skills honed from more than 70 years of living at the helm of leadership in the toughest city and state in the world, New York, New York, USA.

President Trump is exactly the right leader at the right time, preserving America's freedom, ingenuity, the Bill of Rights, and what makes it great, while other countries took the easy (or lazy) way out, either killing/jailing their citizenry (like China) or letting them all flounder and die in total freedom (like Italy).

It seems that anyone and everyone in the Mainstream Media wants to use the Corona Virus tragedy to pile on the People's President, denying him the credit that he is due, and that he has duly fought for, but like a true American CEO, Donald Trump will prevail.

He is cutting through the bureaucratic red tape and allowing experimental drugs to sail through the otherwise bogged down Food and Drug Administration ("FDA"), while tearing through the Internal Revenue Service ("IRS") and U.S. Treasury to issue sizable checks/payments directly to the American people and the nation's small business, as well as forcing the Department of Education ("DOE") to halt/hold off on demanding monthly student loan payments, while turning on his own industry (this is the hallmark of a great leader and man) the real estate business by ordering them all to hold off on evictions and mortgage foreclosures to help and assist and aid the American people and its small business, which he aptly called Athe engine of America.

If there was anyone in America (or the world) that ever doubted the integrity, love for America, and love for its People of President Donald J. Trump, then this should be dispelled completely and totally by his emergent leadership, like a Phoenix from the Ashes, over the past few weeks in his Presidency.

And as Frank Sinatra once said, "The Best Is Yet To Come, And Won't It Be Fine".

Chapter 5

Rage Against The Corona Virus: America (And The World) Needs To Go Back To Work

The truth of the matter is that America (and most of the Western world), with its insanely high living standards and cozy conditions has completely and totally cut its people off from what they actually are, i.e., mammals in the animal kingdom.

Sure, cities, buildings, organized agriculture, and infrastructure are great to buffer against the slings and arrows of outrageous fortune at the hands of Mother Nature, but mankind should never lose sight of the fact that we all need to eat, drink, sleep, breath and reproduce (the last one only if the first 4 are comfortably met).

In the Animal Kingdom, within the wild, when animals don't eat, drink, sleep, or breathe they die.

Whether they are in packs, or on their own, these rules of nature apply.

In the human world, we have developed money, currency, commerce, trade, farming, cities and business to stabilize and make predictable these needs.

But what happens when a civilization is too safe, secure, stabilized, predictable, well-fed, wealthy and safe?

Humans start getting into trouble, and they also get soft, fearful, weak, and lazy, that's what.

If an epidemic like the Corona Virus hit a pack of lions in the sub-Saharan African grassland, does anyone think that the Leader of the Pack would mandate an "all pack quarantine" for 14 days, or 1 month, or even 3 hours?

The answer is a resounding **_NO_**, because "ya gotta eat."

Even if that means some, or many, of those lions would die.

This is just a harsh, sad reality of life.

So to that end, our red-maned President Donald J. Trump is absolutely right when he tells Americans that we need to "Re-Open America for Business," or that "We Need To Go Back To Work."

He is a creature of the wild Animal Kingdom of Humanity, the rare and wildly successful CEO, ie, he is America's "Leader of the Pack."

And he knows, realizes, and understands that, just like in the animal kingdom, this kind of harsh reality could (and probably will) result in some deaths in society.

This is simply the inescapable law of the jungle.

But the Communists/Socialists of American (and global) society are reveling in this time, where they hope that more and more hundreds of millions if not billions of people will look to the "State" to survive, with hand-outs and welfare checks.

Progressives be damned, you can't outwit or tame Mother Nature, no matter how much money or how many college degrees you have.

But the alternative, which is ordering everyone to "stay home" and "self-isolate" is tantamount to "don't hunt," or "don't eat," or "don't fight to stay alive."

To that end, America (and the rest of the world) needs to take a deep breath, heal as best as they can, lay low for the estimated and scientific "viral incubation/healing phase of 14 days," and then get off their collective behinds, take a shower, shave, put on a suit or a dress, go back to work, and re-stimulate the American (and global) economy and international stream of commerce.

CHAPTER 6

Sadly, The African-American Leadership Of The USA Is One Of The Last Serious Internal National Security Risks Facing America

Much has been written about Communist subversion of the United States, that is, the use by America's enemies, both foreign and domestic, of "divide and conquer" tactics, otherwise known as "Salami Tactics," wherein various different factions consisting of "special protected classes" in America get funded, supported, trained, and directed to attack important and essential infrastructure at the roots of the country, in order to weaken and ultimately bring the country down and to its knees.

Without a doubt, one of the last, most mortal of America's wounds has become the most difficult "nut to crack" in order to move the country forward into its much written about existential goal, the "Shining City On A Hill," but that dream can never come into reality until and unless America, and its own Black citizenry, forgive one another and achieve their mutual peace.

It is no secret that nearly every single Intelligence Agency overseas, in nearly each of the planet's 190 nations, has a unit devoted to "Black American" civil and historical strife within the USA since its founding.

This means that everyone "and their mother" around the world knows that one of the greatest, most lethal Achilles Heels of the USA is its Black American population, and most notably, its leadership.

For it is not the average Black American that is to blame for this outrageous behavior as has been seen during these past few days pertaining to the Minneapolis George Floyd-based nationwide riots, it is at once their Black congressmen, senators, police officers, FBI agents, DOJ and DHS employees, federal and state judges, prosecutors, wealthy celebrities, sports stars and entertainers, and their most wealthy, influential, and powerful, both in the public and private sector, that are squarely to blame for the American Black race's epic failure, inability, or non-willingness to move on from the past, successfully integrate, and forgive the country that they call home.

Another problem is that often Black American leadership, if and when they are "called to the mat" about their own corruption allegations, seem to cry foul and blame collective racism to avoid being investigated/charged/prosecuted/convicted.

In fact studies have also shown that African-Americans are pound for pound, more openly racist and hostile to different races and ethnicities than their white counterparts - and this is especially problematic when they are in positions of societal or government power.

Just as Americans and the world blamed Muslim leaders and their religious leader Imams in the wake of 9/11, or the Catholic Church priests/bishops for all of their sex abuse scandals, or the chief executive officers and board of Planned Parenthood for the sins of the extremist third wave feminist movement, or even extremist Zionist leaders such as Meir Kahane or Irv Rubin or Baruch Goldstein of the Jewish Defense League ("JDL") of "Kach" fame, so must the blame for the out of control, sociologically pathogenic, and ultimately destructive behavior by American Blacks be laid at the feet and responsibility of their leadership.

Leaders exist, not only to bask in the sun and glory of their constituent's triumphs, but also to bear the pain and burden of their peoples' foibles and failures.

While Black American leadership are all to eager, it seems, to enjoy the wealth of African American achievement in countless fields of endeavor such as in the sciences, arts, athletics, music, sports, entertainment, finance, medical, and technical fields, they seem to shun or shrink or blame when incidents like the Minneapolis riots take place.

No other race, religion, or ethnicity does this, to such an extent, no matter how much shit that they have to take.

The burning, looting, destroying, terrorizing, murdering, beating, and attacking of Americas diverse groups of people and their businesses, homes, families, livelihoods, as well as their public and private taxpayer-funded infrastructure by Black Americans, wherein they target Asians, Indians, Koreans, Mexicans, Latinos, Whites, Jews, Arabs, Muslims, Christians, and tons of other races/groups in America, because of their own selfish and self-centered collective pain and anger, is altogether unforgivable, untenable, unacceptable, and criminal in nature, at best.

At worst, it is a National Security threat, and could be treated as such by the United States government.

Because it's not just a White v Black matter anymore, it has now become a Black v White/ American/ Arab/ Muslim/ Latino/ Mexican/ Asian/ Jewish/ Christian/ Latino/ Indian/ Korean/ European *et al* matter, wherein Black Americans refuse to be part of the American fabric, or nation.

During these African-American riots, which seem to occur every few years in America (other races/religions/cultures never have these, other than the American Jews, who ironically enough work with/ direct/control/ organize/fund these Black groups), these Blacks collectively seem like they want to destroy and ruin the American nation - well after 500 years of not adjusting to or integrating within the country, maybe it's time that their leadership also looked at themselves and their own behavior, as well.

Because the future and existence of the entire American nation is now at stake, as well as the hopes, dreams, aspirations, families and lives of the other 300 million Americans and their families in the United States of America.

Enough is now, enough.

Even nations such as Liberia , in Africa, were created to offer a voluntary third country where American blacks could go if their experiences in the USA were not to their, or the country's, satisfaction.

But of course that didn't work out very well, and the vast majority of American Blacks remained here, in the USA.

So African-American leadership need to tell their Black constituency to stop trying to destroy the country.

CHAPTER 7

The Global Oligarchs Have Merged With The Global Communists

Well, it's finally happened.

The global oligarchy has now merged with the global communists, and the only losers, will be the vast majority of the planet's masses and middle class.

When one sees major American corporate icons such as the NBA kow-towing to Communist China and their sensibilities, or when Communist China starts passing global laws such as their National Security Law § 38 which subjects any and all global citizens to arrest and incarceration for life, merely for speaking out and/or criticizing the state, you know the game is over, and the jig is up.

The same thing happened at the end of the Soviet Union, when that nation state's leaders and their oligarch minions merged in order to perfect and steal their world's wealth while being protected by the intelligentsia, military, and police, while rupturing the state like a virus.

The same thing is now happening on a global scale.

The world's wealthiest simply don't care about the world's masses, and they have nothing to fear from the state.

The blame squarely falls on the Anti-Trust Divisions of the U.S. Department of Justice and the Federal Trade Commission, who for years (mainly under the Obama administration) allowed Big Tech and other massive monopolies to grow so large and uncontrollable, that they can literally depose or challenge any type of governmental activity to curtail their anti-competitive or dangerous monopoly power to completely and totally dominate the masses.

Trump's Anti-Trust Divisions are no less to blame since we are now 3.5 years into his administration, and he hasn't done anything about this, either (for him, it seems that swelling the economy with unregulated oligarch wealth/power is better than keeping these oligarchs honest, with a consequently smaller Dow Jones Industrial Average).

The head of the Antitrust Division is an Assistant Attorney General for Antitrust appointed by the President of the United States. Since September 2017, the position of Assistant Attorney General for Antitrust has been held by Makan Delrahim. The heads of the FTC Antitrust Division are also equally useless, ineffective, arrogant, and clueless.

True enough, all of those politicians who promised that they would "take on" various monopolies have all "kissed the ring" and instead taken billions of dollars in lobbying costs, consulting fees, speaker fees, and other mechanisms of legalized bribery of state/government officials, all at the expense of the masses and their children.

Meanwhile they are all in the process of riding off into the sunset, while the rest of the world starves and dies off from coronavirus and other possibly man-made/oligarch made/state made laboratory diseases.

Perhaps this coronavirus was just a "dry run," and the real plague killing off the majority of the global population is yet to come, while the wealthy oligarchs "stay home" because they can, similar to how bank robbers like to see what the speed of the cops will be by staging a break-in.

Either way, what the American people have to realize, is that their elected officials will not protect them, and neither will their favorite multi-national corporations/oligarchs, either.

They've chosen whose side they're on, and it's not yours.

Like former President George W. Bush once said while addressing his wealthiest donors, "This is an impressive crowd. The haves and the have mores. Some people call you the elite. I call you my base."

It seems like global, godless, totalitarian government, is just around the corner (months, not years) unless the masses of the world, and especially America, wake up.

Chapter 8

How The Dodd-Frank Bill Is Hastening The USA Towards Communism

One of the hallmarks and bedrocks of Communism is that the state owns and controls all forms of property, and that essentially, private property must be abolished.

So what happens when International Communists encounter a country wherein one of their premier constitutional guarantees is the right to "life, liberty, property" if not the "pursuit of happiness," as paraphrased from the 5th and 14th Amendments.

Well, those international communists would spend billions, if not trillions of dollars, to lobby and place within that country's government, judges, legislators, and executive branch leaders who would work within their own country's system and laws, on the books, to legally and equitably remove any and all forms of private property from their citizenry, gradually and slowly so that no one would really notice and therefore rebel, either in the courts, or the elections, or in the congress/senate.

Well that targeted "country" is the United States of America, and the perfect "crisis" that appeared in 2008, the housing/financial crisis, wholly created when the leftist, socialist, communist mostly permeating within the Democrat party, led by such men as Andrew Cuomo who was then head of the Housing Urban Development ("HUD"), made the obtaining of a mortgage and therefore a home, was so low as to allow any hamburger flipper working minimum wage, with terrible credit history, the ability to buy a million dollar home.

This predictably led to mass mortgage payment failures *en masse*, and when it counted in the tens of millions of homeowners, became a full fledged financial crisis in 2008 which literally threatened to topple the entire United States of America, had these mortgage banks, not been bailed out to the tune of $750 billion dollars in taxpayer dollars, as they were deemed "too big to be allowed to fail."

Enter in the equally draconian, middle of the night, overbearing and over-stretching "Dodd-Frank Bill," of course written and introduced by 2 leftist socialist Democrats, Senator Chris Dodd of Connecticut and Congressman Barney Frank of Massachusetts, which, while cowering behind all of the rules and agencies such as the Consumer Financial Protection Bureau ("CFPB") which was designed to police and regulate dishonest and risky banking behavior, (as well as insurance, credit card, and real estate companies), also put the proverbial "kibosh" on the ability of the average American to purchase and buy a home, by severely raising the cash down payment required to obtain a mortgage (who has up to 55% of the entire home cost in cash in their back pocket, and why would you need a mortgage anyway if that's what's required, as well as having near perfect credit - nearly impossible).

This is a huge case of "throwing out the baby with the bath water," and is fairly typical of American government hysterical reaction to various crises (communist inspired) which usually and often lead to sweeping (usually pre-written) legislation, judicial interpretation, and executive action which brings America and its citizenry closer, and closer to outright Communism and the surveillance state.

Other examples include, but are not limited to, the Patriot Act in the wake of 9/11, or the National Defense Authorization Act of 2014 allowing the U.S. Government to kill American citizens anywhere in the world, without charges or a trial.

Now that the leftist Democrats are in power, in both the Legislature and the Executive Branch, let's see if they can honor their own words, sentiments, and supposed underlying desires to "help low to middle income" Americans by repealing/amending those portions of the Dodd-Frank bill which actively prevent middle class and low income Americans from obtaining a mortgage and buying a home, or let's see if they prefer to relegate those same Middle and Lower Income Americans to renting instead of owning, in line with the Communist Manifesto, with the only ones still owning property being the ruling class of the Communist system, i.e., the Oligarchs, or the Plutocrats, just like in the former Soviet Union ("USSR").

Chapter 9

America's Government Leaders Are By And Large Cowards

The enemies of America have learned some salient things about American leadership and also how easy it is to take over the country, without invasion or even firing a shot.

They have realized that America, with its immense and open lobbying opportunities, the ability to literally buy off and pay for their very own "pet" senators, congressmen, federal and state judges, and myriad members of the executive branch (including the president), that the "boiling frog" approach to taking over and dominating America (and its citizenry) is the best approach, rather than some type of "Red Dawn" nonsense which would galvanize the people, unite them, and force them to cry out *Molon Labe*" while shooting back and sabotaging the newly invading government from mountains and hilltops.

Rather, America's enemies have set aside hundreds of swiss bank accounts, "sweetheart deals" with U.S. Government leaders' family members, business cronies, and friends, and other covert tactics of bribery and coercion to get American leaders to rule the American people with an iron fist, where their votes and sentiments and dreams are purposefully sabotaged and blunted, to mean nothing.

Make no mistake - these foreign enemies, aided by their domestic aiders and abetters (private and public entities) routinely commit grave and horrific acts of violence, civil liberties and human rights violations, the takings of life, liberty, and property in complete and total violation of the 5th and 14th Amendments, going so far as to frivolously and fraudulently remove American citizen's children from them using the family courts and DHS/CPS, locking them up in prisons for crimes that they did not commit, openly surveillancing and monitoring them without their knowledge or permission in gross violation of the 4th Amendment, all in all culling and milking the American people for all that they are worth through taxation without representation, denying them credit and loans to purchase their own property in furtherance of the communist manifesto where the states/oligarchs own everything, and now lately in the last few years, the crushing of their First Amendment rights through the use of massive Big Tech to squelch and silence any dissidence or ideas which would have made the Founding Fathers roll in their graves.

But the problem is, the American peoples' leaders are by and large cowards and traitors - even the "famous ones" that claim to "buck the tide" and "fight the deep state" are more in love with their country clubs, photo ops on FoxNews and CNN, posh and cushy big (and multiple million dollar houses), free perks and jets and "truth finding" vacations to foreign lands, hob-knobbing with the global elite, partaking of the richest and most rare foods and torrid sexual experiences, and other behavior patterns more akin to the leaders of Soddom and Gomorrah, then an American leader, vis-a-vis the men who fought and died to form this country in the 1600s and 1700s to free this land from the yoke of European and international monarchy and tyranny.

This same story happened in ancient Rome, time and time again, when the Roman senators and leadership, arrogantly wearing their purple fringed togas would lord it over the people whom they derided as "plebeians," or "peasants," who would then engage in round after round of revolution over the centuries, in order to re-establish honesty and purity in government, because ancient Roman "patrician" leadership's mistake was openly revealing and allowing their repression, violence, family separation, whippings, beatings, starvation, exploitation, disdain, disrespect, disgust, and oppression of their people to be out in the open - today's American leaders (in all 3 branches) cover the iron first of their abuse of the American people, with subterfuge, false modesty, gentility, and with a proverbial purple velvet glove.

CHAPTER 10

How A Left-Wing Indian Born Immigrant (Barely A U.S. Citizen[1]) Got To Ban Hundreds-Year Long American Citizens And The President Of The United States From Twitter

It's a shame, really.

To become a U.S. Citizen is relatively difficult, but was even more difficult almost 250 years ago when the first Americans fought, died, and shed their blood to free themselves from the tyrannical rule of the British, Europeans and Globalists during the American Revolution.

These American Patriots died in the millions over 250 years to keep and preserve the First Amendment, the right to speak and express ones opinions freely, without censorship, or punishment.

But all it took, was one "useful idiot" by the name of Vijaya Gadde, Chief Legal Officer and General Counsel of Twitter, to help ban them all, and their offspring, and shut them all up, forever in early 2021 under the guise of "public safety."

---

[1] https://ans-wer.com/vijaya-gadde/

According to her Wikipedia page, Vijaya Gadde was born in India to a Telugu family and moved to the United States at age 3. Her father pursued graduate studies in the United States and initially did not have the financial means to send for his wife and daughter until Gadde turned three. Her family moved to Beaumont, Texas. She has described her childhood as having been traumatically "affected" by the Ku Klux Klan presence in Beaumont, so much that her "Indian father was required to get permission from the local Klan before he could go door-to-door for soliciting insurance." So clearly this woman has issues with certain white men and culture.

Gadde received a BS in industrial and labor relations from the Cornell University School of Industrial and Labor Relations and her JD from New York University School of Law in 2000. She later immersed herself for years in the world of Silicon Valley where she presumably was around the Big Tech oligarchs and absorbed their generically globalist attitudes and outlook.

On or about January 14, 2021, Twitter began their purge led by such monsters as Vijaya Gadde by arbitrarily and capriciously suspending user accounts of long time members and American citizens, many of whom never had a problem, or were never even been warned before about any type of misconduct or violation of Twitter's Terms of Service, some who never even wrote original tweets but rather simply retweeted other tweets, mainly from mainstream news media, and wherein some of those banned users were actually victims of online harassment, abuse, and threats from others sharing Vijaya Gadde's professed political views.

Even famous Indian-American U.S. Citizens appeared to be getting targeted based on their ethnicity and politically conservative (Republican) opinions, by other Indians who were born in India who have a leftist, socialist, communist political bent like Twitter's chief counsel, Vijaya Gadde and other of their technical staff, who routinely engage in un-American and un-Constitutional behavior like banning free speech, simply because Twitter is a private company, and not a government institution, thus totally abusing their Communications Decency Act § 230 immunity from complaints/lawsuits, by acting as a "publisher" or otherwise shutting down harmless free speech from conservatives or Republicans, that they do not like.

It is high time that the U.S. Department of Justice Anti-Trust Division, Federal Trade Commission Anti-Trust Division, U.S. Congress and U.S. Senate investigate this abuse of market power, discrimination, and immediately reinstate those suspended accounts, have Twitter apologize for these arbitrary and capricious "suspensions," and have those responsible terminated from employment or investigate the Twitter employees responsible.

CHAPTER 11

Here Comes the United Nations and EU To Save America From Its Deep State, Once Again

Once again, here comes the United Nations ("UN") and European Union/ European Commission ("EU/EC") to save Americans from their Deep State, which has a stranglehold on both them and their psyche.

With the latest (surely reluctant) permission granted to the United Nations by relatively moderate U.S. Secretary of State Antony Blinken, to investigate allegations of widespread and systemic racism and discrimination within the United States of America, and within its public and private institutions, the UN and EU have once again been forced to do the job that the Deep State American Oligarchs either refuse to do, or deny even exists.

The fact of the matter is that the UN and the EU have saved America before, many times, when administrative remedies by oppressed or stifled Americans have been exhausted, all the way up sometimes to the many Circuit and sole U.S. Supreme Court, let alone by the corporate and oligarch funded prostitutes in the U.S. Congress and the Senate.

But most of time the USA Deep State has been very effective in either refusing UN and EU investigation into their alleged war crimes and internal domestic skirmishes, or by simply pulling out of UN and EU related treaties and agreements.

The Executive Branch, consisting of the Presidency, is by far the easiest for the Deep State to control, with money, blackmail, extortion, threats, or mockery by the Deep State controlled Mainstream Press (see the experiences of former President Donald J. Trump).

Americans forget that it was the European Commission on Antitrust, led by the modern day "Joan of Arc" Margrethe Vestager, who first put a "dent" in the sides of Google and other Big Tech communist behemoths, fining and sanctioning them to the tune of hundreds of billions of Euros, when it came to anti-competitive behavior, market manipulation, stifling of competition, organized defamation/slander/libel of Deep State targets, and above all, the wholesale prevention of free speech and expression by those Deep State American oligarchs (but only when the Deep State started to realize that they were also getting victimized by anti-Deep State forces within Big Tech).

This is all the while U.S. Deep State stooges Makan Delrahim, former Antitrust Czar at the U.S. Department of Justice (and former lobbyist for Google) and Ajit Pai, former Federal Communication Commission Chairman (and former legal counsel of Verizon Communications) did virtually nothing while the country burned like Rome as they played the fiddle like Emperor Nero, allowing these two entities to amass even more and more and influence and power under their tenure and watch.

The same thing is happening again - the Deep State is a Master of Manipulation, and has realized that inviting the UN and EU into the USA to investigate systemic racism/discrimination within its public and private institutions could theoretically serve two purposes: (1) to finally shut up their critics accusing them of systemic discrimination with a stamp of approval by the UN/EU (provided that the latter can be controlled/cajoled/ intimidated/extorted/blackmailed/bought off) and (2) to once again find some convenient scapegoat to blame it on (e.g., Black Lives Matter, White Supremacists, Communists, Militias, Immigrants, Immigrant-haters, Radical Islam, whatever).

This is because part of the reason that the Deep State is so effective, is because they never come out into the sunlight themselves - rarely if ever.

However they often wheel out their favorite political/racial faction/group *du jour* whenever they need to accomplish a foreign or domestic policy goal that the vast majority of Americans do not support, vocally.

Hopefully the UN and the EU will not be cowed into submission and produce a sanitized version of what the real problem is - Deep State penetration, complete, and total infiltration of the United States' executive, legislative, and judicial branches of government, from the federal all the way down to the extreme backwoods local.

But the danger is always there, and omnipresent, unless the American people are made aware and welcome this much needed spring housecleaning of the cob-webbed dusty attics of the USA.

It isn't a perfect situation or scenario, but Americans must realize that the reasons that they are frustrated, the reasons that things never seem to change or get done, is entirely because the American Deep State will not allow this change, because they collectively think that they are "better than you."

Former U.S. Supreme Court Justice Louis Brandeis once said in 1914 that "Sunlight is the ultimate disinfectant," and this has been no truer than it is, right now. [2]

---

[2] Louis Brandeis (1914), "What Publicity Can Do", in Other People's Money and How the Bankers Use It: "Publicity is justly commended as a remedy for social and industrial diseases. Sunlight is said to be the best of disinfectants; electric light the most efficient policeman."

CHAPTER 12

American Communism, Like All Social Engineering, Hits Its Minorities First

Mainstream American majorities such as white-Americans, christian Americans, need to understand that Communism always takes the boiling frog approach to mass societal change, but usually their tell-tale signs of mass change is first tested on the USA's minority populations, such as African-Americans, immigrants, unpopular minorities and others who lack a voice in the U.S. Congress, Senate, Judiciary or Executive branches of government.

This way there is really no one to complain when basic civil liberties and fundamental human rights get taken away in the name of state security or safety while mainstream white Americans either don't know what is going on right under their noses, don't care even if they do because it does not necessarily concern them, or even more perversely, support and enjoy it because they harbor deep animosity themselves against those groups.

That is, until those human social engineering experiments become more entrenched and firmly established in American jurisprudence through years and years of judicial interpretation, implementation, and case precedence, as well as those communist sympathizer congress and senate members who venture out of their wretched political caves and kick around and pass legislation designed to either amend or strengthen those communist statutes and laws first usually introduced by one or two bought and paid for leaders in the executive branch (either state or federal).

International global communists have realized that Americans are by and large not interested in the world around them, paying attention only to threats of violence or terrorism against them and their families, but will most likely remain metaphorically asleep when statutes and laws are passed (usually under the guise/cover of a traumatic event, a heart-rendering event, or for general safety).

Some examples of these communist legal changes which have fundamentally transformed America, bringing it closer into the folds of international communism, are:

(1) the Dodd-Frank bill, which was introduced after the 2008 financial crisis, which effectively shuts down the ability of Americans to buy/own a home with a mortgage unless they can pay a minimum of 20% in cash their dream house (used to be 0-5% down if you had good credit) thus keeping private property out of the hands of most Americans;

(2) coronavirus mask-wearing, prohibition of public and private gatherings, psychological conditioning to nameless/faceless governmental submission, experimental vaccination/invasion of body by government;

(3) Patriot Act first brought on by terrorists later revealed to be U.S. intelligence linked operatives now used on all Americans, young and old of every race and gender;

(4) Department of Homeland Security also brought about by 911 terrorists which had its final touches added by former European STASI/KGB kingpin Markus Wolfe who was imported by USA;

(5) installation of communist/socialist activists in the federal/state/local judiciary by similar leaning executive branch members, such as child support magistrates who can jail people in debtors prisons without even a trial or a hearing based on a whim;

(6) countless, innumerable limitless other examples.

They key to maintaining our freedoms as Americans is to self-educate, communicate with one another, hold feed to the fire legally and equitably our elected leaders, whether local, state or federal to enact change and to be held accountable for their refusal (wilful, ignorant or accidental) to protect and defend each and every bit of freedom that our Founding Fathers fought and died for to create and establish the United States Constitution, Bill of Rights, and Declaration of Independence from Europe, whose Oligarchs are still, to this day, trying to pull us back in.

Chapter 13

NYC Mayor Bill De Blasio's Covert Communist Revolution

Recent world events have amply proven and demonstrated the clandestine, quiet, silent Communist revolution taking place in America today, spearheaded and led by international coward and Jewish billionaire terrorist financier George Soros, using the angriest Blacks of America as their foot soldiers.

Yet what most people don't know is that NYC Mayor Bill De Blasio is one of George Soros' best most effective communist revolutionary agents.

This is all the more interesting since George Soros is one of the Rothschild Banking Cartel's best most effective communist revolutionary agents.

To that end, pretty much everything that Bill De Blasio does, is commanded by his boss George Soros, who in turn carries out the will of their ultimate boss, the Rothschild Mafia Family.

During the 1950s, at the height of the Red Scare, both of his parents Maria De Blasio and Warren Wilhelm were accused of having a "sympathetic interest in Communism."

In 1984, de Blasio worked for the Urban Fellows Program at the New York City Department of Juvenile Justice, in 1987, shortly after completing graduate school at Columbia, de Blasio was hired to work as a political organizer by the Quixote Center in Maryland, and in 1988, he traveled with the Quixote Center to Nicaragua for 10 days to help distribute food and medicine during the Nicaraguan Revolution. De Blasio was an ardent supporter of the ruling socialist government, the Sandinista National Liberation Front, which was opposed by the Reagan administration at the time. After returning from Nicaragua, de Blasio moved to New York City, where he worked for a non-profit organization focused on improving health care in Central America.

He continued to support the Sandinistas in his spare time and joined a group called the Nicaragua Solidarity Network of Greater New York, which held meetings and fundraisers for the Sandinista political party.

De Blasio's introduction to city politics came in 1989, when he worked as a volunteer coordinator for David Dinkins' mayoral campaign. Following the campaign, de Blasio was an aide in City Hall. In 1990, he described himself as an "advocate for democratic socialism" when asked about his goals for society. U.S. Representative Charles Rangel tapped de Blasio to be his campaign manager for his successful 1994 reelection bid. In 1997, he was appointed to serve as the regional director for the United States Department of Housing and Urban Development ("HUD") for New York and New Jersey under the administration of President Bill Clinton. As the tri-state region's highest-ranking HUD official, de Blasio led a small executive staff and took part in outreach to residents of substandard housing. In 1999, he was elected to be a school board member for Brooklyn School District 15. The following year, he served as campaign manager for Hillary Clinton's successful United States Senate bid.

Does one have to really wonder who exactly is the NYC white leader nexus for the angry Black foot soldiers of the U.S. Communist revolution on behalf of the Rothschild Banking Family?

Or why Bill De Blasio, year after year, refuses to fire corrupt Black NYC federal/state/family/criminal/civil court judges, socialist/communist administrative workers in NYC government, or within its legislative/ executive branches?

Communist salami tactics (divide and conquer) only work when separate protected class groups such as militant homosexuals, blacks, feminists, and zionists work together towards a common goal - in this case, it's global Communism emanating from the richest, most powerful, most progressive city in the world - New York City - and painting Black Lives Matter across from President Donald Trump's own house on 5th Avenue in Manhattan was Bill De Blasio's crowing symbolic achievement of his Communist Revolution, and neither the New York City FBI Field Office nor the Southern District of New York federal courthouse nor the Manhattan District Attorneys Office will do anything about it, because they have been completely and totally taken over/infiltrated by these exact same Rothschild/Soros/De Blasio Communists.

Therefore United States President Donald Trump is totally powerless against punk NYC Mayor Bill De Blasio, who is backed up by the richest most powerful families and entities that have ever existed in the world.

CHAPTER 14

The Generational Degradation Of Customer Service, Pride In Work And Personal Professional Integrity

A great deal has been written about each and every generation cursing the one(s) coming after their own, always with the same complaints echoing that "things ain't what they used to be," and about how "today's generation" engages in all sorts of cardinal sins, particularly in the customer service industry, the workplace, in business, product quality, even clothing dressing and personal appearance standards.

Even though it is in fact a generational lark, and has been going on in one shape or another for probably thousands of years, there is some truth to these generational critiques and criticisms that as history has shown harkens the impending doom and end to the particular civilization that the "old timers" want so badly to cling to, but a fairly good indication of the esoteric and non-physical/non-visible "fall of civilization" can always be physically and visibly manifested in the slow but painful open deterioration in the above referenced qualities in any civilization.

Some additional physical/visible characteristics exhibited by younger generations of once great civilizations can also include, but are not limited to:

(1) the wholesale abandonment of appropriate clothing for the incident at hand, whether it is work, school, special occasions, restaurants, etc to make way for rags and other disrespectful paraphernalia which could make a peasant of old, wince;

(2) the "mass resignation" so much discussed by various news pundits in the wake of the coronavirus pandemic crisis, wherein millennials and "generation Z" imbeciles find it useful and extremely hilarious to jump from job to job, using and abusing their companies and bosses who routinely invest tens of thousands of dollars, if not millions, in their training, time spent, enduring their inevitable errors and mistakes leading to client/monetary/reputational loss and damage, all the while these generally unappreciative young employees, molded and nurtured heavily on parental and schooling "entitlement feelings" where they can do no wrong and there are no consequences for their negative actions, or even the country they are raised in (mainly a Western society fail) coddle and encourage this type of mass irresponsible behavior as it makes them more dependent on the State (see Oligarchs and Banks) for sustenance and basic living standards, thus transforming them into makeshift slaves wearing symbolic masks to shut their opinions up and stop making waves;

(3) general lack of motivation in young people to embrace or manifest certain value systems which made their previous generational progenitors and their country formerly "great," such as stoicism, loyalty, honesty, respect for others especially leaders and elders who have great experiences to teach, hard work, "going without out" in hope for the future, patience, diligence, steadfastness, postponing immediate pleasure, modesty, and other traits which were previously borne out of necessity by previous generations in order to make their countries great in the first place;

(4) tolerance for the complete and total encroachment on their privacy and trampling over their personal and most basic fundamental civil liberties and human rights, to the point where they feel that since there is no privacy anyway, they publicly act out their innermost demons on a regular basis, thus dragging down society as a whole, or exhibiting such extreme apathy accepting that there is no respect for their human rights, so why should they reciprocate and respect other members of society's civil liberties either;

(5) the wholesale replacement of spirituality, natural inspiration and wholesome gifts bestowed by nature with the countless and multiple trinkets supplied by limitless money, wealth, and mercenary pursuits, junking entire previous generations' previous joys that also provided long term existential fulfilment, but now today's generation constantly "bored" and looking for that next "fix" to catapult them to even higher levels of joy, however dangerous and destructive it may be (dangerous drugs, dangerous sex, risky lifestyle behaviors);

(6) the rejection of marriage and family, in favor of multiple sex partners of every variety and number, shunning and avoiding any type of long-term relationship as a "threat to their identity and/or freedom," while all that does is create greater dependence on the State for stability, monetary support, and basic assistance.

If one has not figured it out already, all of the above attributes of a deteriorating and degrading society have one destination for the people of that country - and that is Totalitarianism/Communism, i.e., the complete and utter control and enslavement of the masses, by the few fortunate ones with the power who make up the "State."

More politicians, congressmen and senators, especially the nation's judges and executive branch, should be paying greater attention to this mass societal deterioration falling and occurring all around them in implementing their policies and laws, otherwise there is no reason why the United States of America (or other countries undergoing similar breakdown) will not follow the empires of past into the dirt and ground, for the last tens of thousands of years.

CHAPTER 15

American Communism's "Frank Serpico" Method Of Eliminating Dissidents

American law enforcement (federal, state and local) knows very well that the average American is a victim of crime more often than anyone could possibly imagine, especially in light of the Lavrenty Beria/Felix Dzerzhinsky-like communist police state that we all now currently live in, wherein almost anything and everything is illegal, or can be construed as illegal, given the right "legal massage" administered by your everyday average corrupt cop, district attorney, prosecutor, investigator, or anyone with the power to investigate, charge, prosecute and convict.

That's why they know that violently eliminating political dissidents, or "enemies of the state," through beatings/murder *a la* the former Soviet Union or NAZI Germany is wholly unnecessary in today's modern day American communist state, and with the advent of rampant, active and boisterous social media updates right to the second, they probably could not get away with killing off their enemies like in the "good old days of yore," even with slow methods like inflicting cancer artificially, heart attacks, biological and chemical diseases, etc.

To that end, the leaders of the American Communist revolution have instead resorted to a uniquely American-style of killing off their targets, using a method that we can henceforth call the "Frank Serpico," or simply, the "Serpico Method."

Casual students of American criminal history (especially that of New York City, the hotbed and origin of American-style Communism) will fondly recall the tragic story of NYPD Police Officer Frank Serpico, who as legend has it, was one of the only honest police officers on the force of the burgeoning corrupt and communist New York City Police Department back in the 1960s and 70s, when that force was undergoing its transformation from a force rife with honest good police officers, but that later became chock full of lying, dishonest cops who were "on the take" from the Oligarchs, Organized Crime, and New York City money powers that be, i.e., the founders of American Communism.

As retaliation for bringing down the largest number of corrupt dirty police officers within the NYPD by testifying against them, Frank Serpico was "rewarded" by his superiors by being sent into violent drug dens with little to no back up, where eventually he wound up getting shot in the face, all the while his "partners" stood there on the sidelines of the door, passively watching.

These lying deceitful police officers, together with their Communist Oligarch masters, would later smoothly and sinuously normalize police corruption under the thin veneer of blue colored efficiency and organization.

But the bad habits, such as retaliation, murder, false arrest/incarceration, institutionalized deceit, and above all, serving their "Masters" never changed or waivered, it just became part of the rules promulgated therein.

Recently, even the Internal Affairs Bureau of the NYPD became embroiled and exposed as simply an arm of NYPD organized crime, running prostitution, narco-trafficking, murder for hire, and other sick acts typical of the mafia rather than a police department.

Sure enough, the federal authorities quickly followed suit, and then this cancer spread throughout the United States, and on into the other branches of government, the legislative and executive, again, beholden to and working for their American oligarch communist masters.

Returning to the original theme of this article, the "Serpico" method that the American Communist government uses is simply this:

Just ignore, or do not investigate, or "shit can" the *bona fide*, legitimate criminal complaints of your Communist Oligarch Masters' targets/enemies, and let the criminals do their job against your targets.

That way, one presumably as "clean hands," and does not actively partake in the extortion, blackmail, harassment, aggravated harassment, threats, intimidation, murder, beatings, robbery or other violence against your targets, like the Communist thugs of the former Soviet Union or NAZI brownshirts/Gestapo used to inflict on their targets, making it "government sponsored criminal activity."

The Oligarchs of today have learned that when they lose their moral authority, or are suspected of doing so, that their reign quickly comes to and end, like it did in those 2 regimes, either through outright war by other nations, or regime change from within.

Indeed, even the formerly incorruptible United States Supreme Court has been infected with the Communist bug in that they have now institutionalized this "Frank Serpico" method of policing/regulation/elimination of political dissidents/enemies of the Oligarchs/State, with their ruling in cases such as DeShaney vs. Winnebago and Town of Castle Rock vs. Gonzales, wherein the once coveted United States Supreme Court has ruled that police agencies are not obligated to provide protection of citizens.

In other words, police are well within their rights to pick and choose when to intervene to protect the lives and property of others — even when a threat is apparent.

Even more sickeningly, and further underscoring the absolute sadistic nature of American Communist Oligarchs and Rulers, in both of these court cases, clear and repeated threats were made against the safety of children — but government agencies chose to take no action.

"Neither the Constitution, nor state law, impose a general duty upon police officers or other governmental officials to protect individual persons from harm — even when they know the harm will occur," said Darren L. Hutchinson, a professor and associate dean at the University of Florida School of Law.

"Police can watch someone attack you, refuse to intervene and not violate the Constitution."

The Supreme Court has repeatedly held that the government has only a duty to protect persons who are "in custody," he pointed out.

Thomas Jefferson was a very big proponent of educating the masses so that they can remain free from the claw-back by the European-based Oligarchs and Communist Slavemasters after Americans won their freedom in the American Revolution and the Declaration of Independence in 1776.

Well, this is one area of modern day policing and regulation, that the American People really need to pay attention to.

CHAPTER 16

Some Controversial Truisms
(That Many Don't Want You To Know)

(1) There is no "Deep State" - it's just mainly dominated by organized Jews;

(2) Whatever name you give it, "communists," marxists," "deep state," "leftists," "illuminati," "freemasons," "socialists," "antifa," "oligarchs," "elites," whatever, it's really just organized Jews led and directed by their Rabbis in their individual synagogues - those organizations may have plenty of non-Jews in them, but at the end of the day the Jewish members, through their leadership, using force, trickery, gangstalking, bullying, money, bribery, corruption, harassment, intimidation, threats, blackmail, extortion, violence, manipulation, guilt, eventually and ultimately dominate and transmit those organizations' messages, platforms and political positions;

(3) Some Blacks are perfectly capable (and often do) engage in organized racism, discrimination, oppression, unfairness, and cruelty often times when they are in federal, state and local government (judicial, executive, legislative) when there are enough of them in power (usually the major cities), and many of them communicate with each other to ruthlessly and relentlessly

(and unconstitutionally) discriminate against others, mainly conservative or Republican minorities, poor (non-Jewish) whites, and anyone else that their political overlords (mainly organized Jews) do not like, or hate;

(4) "It's mainly organized wealthy Jews and their leadership, at the source and bottom of most societal problems facing global humanity today.

Chapter 17

Most Government Regulatory Agencies Are Designed To "Shit-Can" Legitimate Complaints

The oligarchs, bankers, civil rights violators, big tech mavens, insurance companies, and credit card merchant service companies across the United States have discovered that getting sued by an angry litigant is a lot more dangerous than receiving a "complaint" from the various "regulatory agencies" such as the Consumer Financial Protection Bureau, New York State Department of Financial Services, New York State Division of Human Rights, and especially the New York State Attorney General, because these agencies are by and large staffed by the dumbest, laziest, most corrupt government workers that could ever exist.

A massive investigation needs to take place by a federal agency or congressional or senate committee to trace the obscene amounts of bribe money that flows from these massive plutocratic civil and human rights violators down to the wallets and bank accounts of the government staff workers inside these agencies, as well as to their friends, families, and business cronies, because this level of corruption is unprecedented in American history.

It's to the point where the only hope that a complainant can seek justice is by preparing and filing his own lawsuit, or have the money to hire a lawyer, by taking the matter into his or her own hands, legally and equitably.

Because nothing at all will occur, of any consequence if an American citizen places his faith in these governmental regulatory agencies whose only job seems to be gaslighting and humiliating the complainants, obstructing justice, obfuscating the issues, and otherwise muddying the proverbial waters so that truth and justice are buried deep down into the equally proverbial riverbed.

This is why socialism and communism does not work, because of corrupted governmental worker idiots like this.

Chapter 18

Lets Face It – Many American Women Are Only Getting Worse

Many American (and now global) women don't even try to hide it anymore - in social settings, in the workplace, in restaurants and nightclubs, many women are now fully baring their talons, and are make no bones about their inherent predator aspects - and their prey is the true, honest, loyal, supportive balanced male.

For these con-artist American women, having been emboldened by the fraudulent #MeToo movement, and armed with their special protected class status handed to them by the 1994 VAWA law, make no bones about what their true intentions and feelings about today's modern day man is - to seize their assets and subjugate them cruelly underneath their Christian LeBoutin high heeled shoes.

They use love as a tool and weaponize romance - they cull and cultivate their prey using sex, submission, feckless agreeing that today's women are all bad, and try and resonate with their male victims - but only temporarily.

This is their method of disarming, defanging and softening up their male victims before lowering the guillotine around their necks, usually after the requisite period of time elapses when they have made their victim's home, their home.

Then the fun starts - threats, blackmail, extortion, coercion, and subtle reminders that they have the power to arrest that man at will simply by calling 911 and lying.

To these types of women, Love is now a foregone conclusion - sex immediately stops or becomes less frequent, openly cheating with and texting other men becomes more pronounced and obvious, disrespecting their male victims becomes par for the course (either alone or with their friends/family), and liberties begin to be taken with their male victim's credit cards, money, resources, skills, talents and above all, patience.

As soon as their male victim wakes up from his metaphorical slumber and notices that things have gone horribly wrong, and tries to once again gain his self-respect back, the game is over - that woman could now start to record him during arguments, provoke and inflame him further, and then calmly tell him that she has him threatening her on tape.

An automatic arrest.

The extortion game has now fully begun, and the hapless now psychologically neutered male victim is now hopelessly trapped, unable and totally clueless as to how to cut himself free, without the prospect of losing everything he owns or worked for.

If he calls the police first, he runs the risk of getting arrested himself, with that women obtaining a restraining order and his entire house to herself, free to bring over all of those men that she's been texting/communicating with while jeering in his face.

These horrific con-artist type woman have now become quite common in modern day American society.

More attention needs to be spent on this topic by Congress, Senate, the Judiciary, and the Executive Branch.

CHAPTER 19

Many of Today's Women Need To Come With Warning Labels

Now that modern day society has forced humankind to obtain licenses for carrying virtually every type of weapon imaginable, it is now only fitting that today's modern day woman, having now been thoroughly brainwashed to "weaponize" their sexuality with the assistance of Joe Biden and Bill Clinton's draconian unconstitutional VAWA law sponsored and pushed by organized feminism, incarcerating or ruining the life of any man at will, for any reason, even if there is no evidence, that women now be required to state their intentions and just who they are, up front.

It is no secret to men that have slept with many women, universally report that a great majority of women appreciate and prefer a man that "takes control," in life, as well as sexually, as a formal and open display of their manhood and societal dominance.

Indeed, most woman report that nothing turns off the vast majority of them than a sniveling, cowardly, unconfident man that can't make decisions and act in a forthright, direct manner.

But the small minority of angry women calling themselves feminists have completely hijacked the women's movement through psuedo-CIA and western intelligence mechanisms and front groups like the National Organization of Women ("NOW"), Planned Parenthood, and other extremist feminist hate groups, who falsely screech and claim that

59

basically all sexual acts and interpersonal relationships by and between men and women within their families, relationships, corporate working environments, and every other arena of human interaction are characterized by violence, abuse, disrespect, hostility and criminality.

It is also no secret that these "women's organizations" are funded and controlled by predominantly male oligarch entities to suspend male civil rights and liberties, and to destroy the nuclear family to make everyone (men, women, and their children) more dependent on the state (which they control), in every capacity.

So it should not be surprising or shocking to the conscience that men should be able to know, in advance, if the woman that they are dating or working with, is either one of the vast majority of females who appreciate strength, dominance, and chivalry, or if they in fact prefer a *beta* male that would never *think* of offending a woman, if even slightly.

One novel but sadly hilarious idea would be the color coding of women's driver licenses, a completely **_voluntary_** decision by that women, to indicate if she likes aggressive, dominant, decisive men, or if she is on the other side of the spectrum, preferring "cuck-like men," who are only a few steps from being girls, themselves.

The color codes for these women's ID cards could theoretically go from preferring "red" (dominant) all the way to preferring "blue" (submissive), with varying degrees of hues in between, indicating their preference.

This forensic self-identifying voluntary information could then be used as only one of the "mitigating factors" tending to exonerate an otherwise innocent male against an opportunistic, nasty, fraudulent woman who intends to nail that man to the wall in the case of a possible divorce proceeding, child custody or visitation battle, in family court, or in a criminal case where that woman intends to impugn the integrity and character of that targeted male to rob and destroy him in those court proceedings.

This "color-coded" ID system could also help men avoid women that are trouble-makers from the get-go, instead of potentially wasting months, if not years, of being "duped" into thinking and believing that the woman that he is with is the "greatest thing since sliced bread," only to have the equally proverbial "rug pulled out from under him" if and when things go south.

This type of color-coding self-identification would go miles to save the males, ensure family integrity, defend against false or spurious allegations of domestic abuse or violence, and ultimately would ensure transparency for all parties involved, and to avoid future disagreements and unpleasantness in the future, saving the courts and the world trillions of dollars in unnecessary costs and heartache.

Chapter 20

Extremist Feminists Have Turned All Heterosexual Men Into Rapists

The very nature of the sexual act by and between men and women is a penis penetrating inside of the vagina.

By its very nature, men must enter the inner sanctum sanctorum of the female body by inserting their body into theirs.

This act has occurred since time immemorial, right from the unicellular organisms of the primordial soup from which life actually arose, and all that has changed is that uni-cellular organisms have organized themselves into multicellular organisms to ensure survival and to reproduce their genetic DNA.

Although it would be quite comical, one can now almost envision a rabid man-hating feminist of the modern age chastising and berating a one celled organism for having the audacity and gumption to have actually inserted its pseudopod into a neighboring one celled organism in order to inject its DNA inside in order to merge DNA, and to produce another one celled organism.

True, human beings have the power to reason, and therefore to consent (or not consent) to sexual encounters, but the rabid feminist movement has taken it too far, to the point where now college students all around the United States must have a signed consent form before they engage in sexual intercourse.

But the polls tell us a different truth - the vast majority of women in the world prefer a strong, dominating, aggressive male because they feel more protected and safe, and the least aggressive, dominating and beta males usually wind up alone.

But organized extremist feminism, which is in reality a tiny minority of the female population, has actually hijacked women and their feelings about sex and relationships.

This is because organized extremist feminism, like other "protected classes," have been openly (and clandestinely) funded and supported by the oligarchs who desperately want to control all people, lock stock and barrel, and what better method than controlling the sexual impulse?

This is the closest thing to acting like God on Planet Earth than human beings will ever come close to. (1 Thessalonians 4:3-7).

The Luciferian oligarchs reason that, if one can control the actual sexual instinct, one can control the entire human race.

This is why they invest in organized extremist feminism, lesbianism, and idiot short-sighted politicians and celebrities who criminalize the very act of sex, right from dating all the way to marriage.

Because the power to criminalize is the power to control.

It is very important that men begin to organize themselves and push back against organized extremist feminism for their own sake, and the sake of their families and children.

Otherwise they are all just sitting ducks, ready to be arrested and taken out of society whenever they fall out of line within the Luciferian paradigm.

Resistance will be futile, and their incarceration/murder will be inevitable, since the only act that follows the necessary human necessity to both breath and eat, is the act of sex.

Imagine if breathing and eating became criminalized/regulated by the Luciferian?

Well that's not a very far cry off, given the circumstances.

Men must begin to push back against this "organized extremist feminist sexual revolution," and begin to advocate to their congress and senate to once again hold hearings on what "consent" means, what "sexual intercourse" means, and also to prescribe severe punishments against women (and men) who falsely claim rape or other sexual abuse.

Men must raise the legal and equitable bar for what defines "rape" or "sexual assault," since the consequences of getting arrested and/or convicted of such an allegation is more heinous than any other criminal allegation in life.

And since it has now become so arbitrary, no man is safe.

And this is no way to live.

CHAPTER 21

Jewish Female Dominated Feminism Has Transformed American Women Into Depressed Diseased Drug Addicted Whores

While Jewish women predominantly and routinely enjoy a nuclear family, replete with a husband whom she takes care of and dotes over, expecting the same level of commitment from her husband, generally dutifully raising her children and running the household, supporting her husband in his workplace, and steadfastly loyal throughout, these Jewish women become "feminazis" as soon as they leave their households and interact with non-Jewish women and men (the Goyim, or non-human "cattle" in Hebrew)".

This is because generally, Jews by nature, because their Rabbis have brainwashed them since birth that they are the "chosen people", hate competition, and want to be the only ones on the block with a healthy and balanced family, while poisoning and advocating behavior and characteristics to the "goyim" (non-Jewish) community about the "female virtues" of complete and total independence from a man, freedom, rampant promiscuity and drug use (anti-depressants and anti-anxiety medication are their favorite prescribed drug of choice for young, white women so that they can become compliant sex and employee slaves for their Jewish husbands), running away from marriage/relationships/commitment as "oppressive," and other such destructive crap.

The end result, with predominantly Jewish oligarchy domination of the 24/7 media, television and the movies, is an entire generation or 2 of American women who are hopelessly drug-addicted, ravaged with disease from the sheer amount of promiscuous unsafe and drug induced sex that they have, psychologically and mentally ruined from the countless sexual relationships they have had, totally isolated and insecure due to no meaningful male (or female) relationships in their lives, emotionally deadened by the time they reach their mid-20s due to the above described behavior, totally untrusting, untrustworthy, and unable to trust anyone, vulnerable to sexual predators, incapable of becoming good and healthy mothers, afraid of marriage, and addicted to money for sex as a means to earn a living.

These women have become literal vermin, diseased harlots doomed to walk the night alone and destroyed.

Russian President Vladimir Putin has seen what 70 years of predominantly Jewish-created and controlled Communism, with its God-less ways, literally destroyed the souls of Russian women and families, when it pushed out God and Christianity from the minds of men and women.

This is why he re-introduced Christian Patriarch Kirill back into an advisory role in his new Russian Federation government, which he began to build back when he took power in 2000 from the drunken Boris Yeltsin, who himself took over after 70 years of Communism began to fall in 1989, after the Russian Communist (predominantly Jewish) Oligarchs had already thoroughly looted and raped the country of its wealth, riches, culture, families, and integrity of its women for 70 years since the October Communist Revolution of 1917.

America desperately needs to be re-calibrated on its moral compass once more, and Christianity, while not literally becoming the law of the land, should also have some type of advisory role in the United States, just like Putin re-instituted in his home country of Russia.

Unfortunately the mainly Jewish Neo-Con Communists of America have slowly and methodically removed and extricated any and all Christian values from the United States, replacing it with Luciferianism and hedonism.